MW01531322

The Trials and Treasures of Life

The Trials and Treasures of Life

Naomi Tomlinson

Copyright © 2014 by Naomi Tomlinson.

| ISBN: | Softcover | 978-1-4990-7290-7 |
| | eBook | 978-1-4990-7289-1 |

All rights reserved. No part of this book may be reproduced or transmitted in any form or by any means, electronic or mechanical, including photocopying, recording, or by any information storage and retrieval system, without permission in writing from the copyright owner.

Any people depicted in stock imagery provided by Thinkstock are models, and such images are being used for illustrative purposes only.
Certain stock imagery © Thinkstock.

This book was printed in the United States of America.

Rev. date: 09/22/2014

To order additional copies of this book, contact:
Xlibris LLC
1-888-795-4274
www.Xlibris.com
Orders@Xlibris.com
668547

CONTENTS

POEMS AND SHORT STORIES
By Naomi Tomlinson

Contentment 13

A Chaplain's Job 14

A Deep Regret 15

A Simple Thank You 16

A Trip To The Nursing Home 17

Along The Way 18

At Conemara 19

Christmas Eve 20

Disappointed 23

Don't Cry For Me 25

Don't Spread Your Woes! 26

Grandma's Advice 27

Grandma Thought Tweet Was A Bird 28

Great Grandma Observes 30

Harper, After Hearts For Hearing 32

Hometown Visit 33

How Did I Fail? 34

I Hate Thin Walls 35

Leaving The Nest 36

Logan, My Five Year Old Great-Grandson 38

Memories Of Graduating Seniors 40

My Friend 42

My Getaway 43

Never Say, How Are You? 44

No Remorse 45

Noble Sacrifice 46

Nostalgic Thoughts Of Winter And Fall 48

Passing Times..50
Preview For Heaven 51
Respectful Decline 52
Sacrifices 54
Some Mother's Son...56
Suddenly, I'm Old 58
Temporary 59
That Certain Smile 60
The Beauty Of Her Smile 61
The Death Of Our Class Comedian 62
The Quiet Man...63
The Simple Life.. 64
They Still Dance 65
Too Late? 66
To Whom Much Is Given 67
Together At Last..68
Too Much Fun 70
Trip To Sandburg's Home 71
Unexpected Love..73
Why? 75
Hard But Necessary Changes 76
The Games We Used To Play 81
I Red Rover..82
II The Needle's Eye 83
III Go In And Out The Windows..................................84
IV Three Deep..86
V Ball And Jacks 87
VI Jumping Rope 88
VII Bobbing For Apples 89
VIII Roll The Hoop...90
IX Barrel Walk And Barrel Ride....................................91

POEM
By Leroy Dority

My Wife..95

POEM
By Lori Eikel

My Brother's House...99

POEMS AND SHORT STORIES
By Judy Goodspeed

For Better Or Worse...105
Mama Tried 107
A Stinky Adventure 109

POEM
By J.D. Hess

Love's Tempest 115

SHORT STORIES
By Johnnie Wingo

Learning The Language 118
Sharecropper's Daughter..122

Dedication

I would like to dedicate this book to my daughter Jennie and her husband Harold Gordon, and to my son Fred McKinney.

Also to my grandchildren: Lindsey Sanders and husband Billy; Whitney Laramore and husband Bryan; Shawn McKinney and wife Beth; and to my granddaughter Teresa Bynum.

This book is really a continuation of my first book The Rhymes and Rhythms of my Life.

I feel blessed and pleased by the response to my first book.

I have written poems and stories since I was a child, however, I showed them to few people until later in life.

In the 80's I began attending writers' workshops. I received much encouragement, but not until 2002 did I become serious. With Judy Goodspeed's encouragement I joined PAWS, a writer's club.

Very soon, I began getting a few things published and I won a few contests.

I will always be grateful to my friend Judy who herself is a writer.

I am also appreciative of my friends at the First Baptist Church.

A very special thank you to my great pals Judy Goodspeed and Johnnie Wingo. Without you this book would never have come into fruition.

Poems And Short Stories

By Naomi Tomlinson

Contentment

I'm living the life fate dealt me,
    Sad but not bereft.
Don't waste your time with sympathy.
    For me, much more is left.

I have great friends and family,
    A perfect place to live,
A faith in God, a place to serve
    And means with which to give.

Sometimes when things do not go well
    I may feel a bit blue,
And though old age comes creeping up,
    I still have much to do.

Many rich blessings come from God
    To me each single day,
And for these gifts that I receive,
    I never can repay.

So when my Savior calls me home
    To meet Him face to face,
There at his feet I'll worship Him
    And thank Him for His grace.

A Chaplain's Job

He softly knelt beside her chair.
    He said I feel your pain.
She didn't try to hide her tears
    For the son who'd been slain.

He was only a child she said.
    Why did he have to go?
And did he die in vain she asked
    I'd really like to know.

With breaking heart, he asks himself
    What can I do or say.
What comfort can I bring to her
    To take her pain away.

A Deep Regret

Today, I saw a small obit
    Tucked in the paper there.
A childhood friend had died last week,
    I don't remember where.

Well, I received a call from her
    About ten years ago.
She said "Why don't you come to lunch?
    It's not so far, you know."

A busy life I led back then.
    My time was always short.
Proudly, I would prioritize,
    But always time was short.

I truly planned to meet with her
    Just for a little lunch,
But of those things which took my time,
    Ever there was a bunch.

So then one day I thought to call,
    But found she'd moved away.
Oh yes, I feel a deep regret.
    I wish I'd gone that day.

A Simple Thank You

A simple "thank you" does not serve
　　My feelings to portray.
I've searched for other words, but then
　　What more is there to say?

Your kindness astounds me!
　　You're loved by everyone.
From the first time that I met you
　　Our friendship had begun.

You go about your daily work
　　Alert to every need.
Amid the sad and lonely ones
　　You sow the kindness seed.

Again, I would like to say thanks
　　For things you do for me,
But I have already told you,
　　So let's just let it be.

A Trip To The Nursing Home

The lonely patients sitting there
    All wrapped up in a quilt.
To those whose loved ones seldom come,
    Do you not feel the guilt?

To some, it only takes a smile,
    Or maybe a light touch.
Children, can you not spare the time?
    It doesn't take that much.

Remember that you, too, some day
    May be the one who's there.
Do you want to be all alone
    And have no one to care?

Along The Way

The river gleams so very bright
In the golden, morning sunlight.

Come walk with me along the way
So I'll not feel alone today.

Now, as we feel the soft breeze,
Sunlight spears the rustling leaves.

And if, by chance, my hand you hold,
I'll feel the warmth and not be cold.

Oh, my sweet, what do you say?
Come walk with me along the way.

At Conemara

A winding ribbon of chat
Took us to a large white fortress
Standing proud in its isolation.

We stepped inside to find unvarnished pine
floors
And naked windows.
Myriad shelves clutched his time worn books
Holding strips of newspaper to mark his
reading places,
And bits of leaves and acorns accessorized his
writing table.

Carrying his orange crate desk
Often he'd mount the pine needle path to Old
Glassy,
Trudging past the goat stables and blue bird
houses of rough wood
Nailed unadorned on old fence posts.

There far removed from human society,
He'd perch his typewriter on his
Homemade desk
And pound out his message
To the common man.

Christmas Eve

It's Christmas Eve and cold outside.
The night is clear and bright.
The lovely trees contain no breeze.
No people cross my sight.

Does no one care I ask myself,
If I'm alive or ill?
Does no one see the bright candle
Upon my window sill?

Outside the snow is thick and deep.
I'll sit here by the fire
And think of times so long ago
While listening to the choir.

Then one by one the pictures flash
Across my memory:
One Christmas Eve the little ring
He proudly gave to me.

I'll think of times when Grandma came
To spend the night with us.
The one night when we all went
To bed without a fuss.

There was something magic about
Those nights on Christmas Eve
When all of us would gather round
His blessings to receive.

Together we all went to church
Where ringing bells we heard
Familiar carols then we sang
And listened to God's word.

Oh, yes there was a closeness there
Among our family.
The joy and peace that once we knew
Live on in memory.

Oh my, is there someone outside
My door this time of night?
What is that knocking that I hear?
It gives me quite a fright.

Then joyfully I hear you call,
Grandma, we came for you.
We could not get you on the phone.
So what were we to do?

We could not leave you all alone
On this most special night.
No holiday would be complete
Without you in our sight.

Looking around we found for you
Outside in Grandpa's shed
The very thing we need tonight.
You see we've found a sled.

We'll all team up and take turns
Pulling you in the sled.
We have a blanket for you and
A pillow for your head.

Precious children, how could I doubt
The love you have for me,
The love begun so long ago
In this, our family.

Disappointed

At six, you were so quiet and meek
    A lovely little child.
To questions asked, you always gave
    Answers so soft and mild.

I watched you during teen-aged years
    Observed your first romance,
But from the time it all began
    It never had a chance.

You ran with ones too young and wild.
    You just followed the crowd.
Things you did, places you went
    Should not have been allowed.

When many years later we met,
    I hoped that things had changed.
So when you came here for a job,
    I had it all arranged.

I remembered that little girl
    The one who was so sweet.
I knew not of your later life,
    Perhaps one on the street.

You asked if I would recommend
    You for this simple job,
But how was I to ever guess
    You'd just come here to rob?

I believed in and trusted you.
　　　I know you're not all bad.
To learn they have arrested you
　　　This makes me very sad.

Well, tomorrow I will call you,
　　　But what am I to say?
What happens next is up to you.
　　　All I can do is pray.

Don't Cry For Me

Don't say that I look natural
    When I am lying dead.
Just realize that I'm not there
    For my spirit has fled.

Shed a few tears if you should wish,
    Scatter flowers around,
Then close the lid on my casket
    And put me in the ground.

Don't weep and wail and cry for me.
    Don't dwell on things long past.
Just feel happy and know that I'm
    Secure with God at last.

Don't Spread Your Woes!

Much of life is tragedy, but
    Through suffering we grow.
Only God can feel your pain.
    No one else needs to know.

Grandma's Advice

Borrowing leads to sorrowing
    My Grandma used to say.
If you'll just spend less than you earn,
    There'll be no rainy day.

Oh, my children listen to me
    For grandmas have hindsight,
So, if you follow my advice
    You're sure to turn out right.

Grandma Thought Tweet Was A Bird

What did you do for fun, Grandma?
　　　Was life dull and a bore?
No telephone nor internet,
　　　Surely you wished for more.

In the evenings with no T.V.
　　　You had no videos!
Whatever did you do at night?
　　　Just went to bed I s'pose.

You couldn't even text your friends—
　　　You say you did not tweet.
How did you keep in contact with
　　　Your friends across the street?

Ah, my dear our life back then
　　　Was very far from dull.
Busy we were with work and play
　　　Each night and day were full.

We fed the chickens, milked the cows
　　　Did many chores each day,
And yet, we knew there'd always be
　　　A time for rest and play.

Our father taught us how to play
　　　A game called "kick the can."
He built us stilts and then we walked
　　　Around like a tall man.

With a ball mother made with yarn
    We played anti-over.
In summer we'd swim or stroll
    Through fields of sweet clover.

Active we were in winter time
    We always had such fun
When dripping trees crackled with ice
    The sledding had begun.

So when the snow fell nice and deep,
    The snowball fight we had
And if we got hit with a ball,
    No one ever got mad.

As teens, we sometimes took sleigh rides,
    And if we had a date,
Out in the pasture was a pond
    Where we could go to skate.

After supper sometimes we'd have
    A cup of hot cocoa.
Our dad would pray with us and then,
    Off to bed we'd go.

Great, Grandma, Observes

Where will you be, my little ones
    When you too, have grown old?
Did you follow in your parents' steps,
    Or have you broken the mold?

I want for you so very much
    More than I ever had.
But then again when I think back
    My life was not half bad.

We had a childhood filled with joy
    And everything was free.
Yes, we could run and sing and play
    Or even climb a tree.

Water was pure, the air was clean
    And one could see the sky.
A true blue, as snow white clouds
    Seemed to be floating by.

Sometime we had a grapevine swing
    Down near a river bank.
There once we made a raft with logs,
    A boat that never sank.

No fear we felt of pedophiles,
    The doors were seldom locked.
No one was scared if after dark
    Someone came up and knocked.

Children, I ask you will you please
Put computers away.
Leave the TV and go outside,
And plan to spend the day.

As I watch you, I ask myself
What will your future bring?
Will you have much to celebrate?
Will you take time to sing?

I hope you have the privilege
To serve your fellow man
And if this brings you happiness
You'll know it is God's plan.

Harper, After Hearts, For Hearing

With hair of gold and eyes of blue
    Our tiny baby girl
Had smiling lips, but puzzled eyes.
    She viewed her noiseless world.

Oh, how we loved and shielded her.
    Then her first birthday came—
And as we asked for a miracle,
    We prayed in Jesus name.

So silent and still was she,
    Our little baby girl.
Then we received the miracle
    That gave our hearts a whirl.

A marvel beyond our wildest dreams
    This child did now receive
And that our God is in control
    We truly do believe.

Once silent, now this little sprite
    Can laugh and talk and sing.
So as we watch her as she plays
    Our thankful hearts do ring.

Hometown Visit

Watch that little old lady there
    As she walks down the street.
Many people pause to meet her.
    Her smile is very sweet.

They ask, How is my old teacher?
    She says, Tell me your name.
They say, We're so glad to see you.
    She answers, Glad you came.

She's puzzled as she walks away
    For she can barely see.
She says, I wonder who they meant.
    Suppose it could be me?

Her son steps up to take her arm.
    He guides her to their car.
She asks, Where are we going now?
    He answers, It's not far.

Slowly, they leave their old home town.
    She says, I loved it all.
You know, I think I once lived here,
    But when, I don't recall.

How Did I Fail?

(A mother, after a son's suicide)

Why, why, my sad heart calls to you
Why did you choose this way?
Why could I not have died instead
And kept your pain at bay.

I long to hold you in my arms
And wipe away your tears.
Could I but turn the sad years back,
I'd chase away your fears.

Was life really all that bad?
Why was there so much pain?
Was there no sunshine in your life?
Just only storms and rain?

Oh, could my blinded eyes not see?
The hidden signs were there.
When silent signs called out to me,
Did I take the time to care?

Was my life filled with only things
Of little consequence?
Was it neglect or busy days?
I've wondered ever since.

I Hate Thin Walls

Next door some people just moved in.
    Last night I heard her cry.
I heard him seem to comfort her.
    This made me wonder why.

I told myself, "Stay out of this,"
    But my walls are so thin!
I tried not to overhear,
    But there it went again.

"Darling, I don't want to lose you,"
    I heard her softly say.
"It's only for a little while," he said,
    "That I must go away."

"I can't bear it for you," she wailed.
    Then she started to cry.
"We'll get through this together, Dear,
    I'm not afraid to die."

Leaving The Nest

You'll not come home again.
I know that now.
I've hidden my sadness
From you somehow.

When I came for a visit,
I expected to see
Homesickness and malcontent.
You surprised me.

Nestled here in the mountains
You've planted a home
Your children and wife are happy
You seem to belong.

You've made me feel welcome.
One thing you'll never know-
That for your mother to keep you
She had to let you go.

I'm going home tomorrow
So many miles away
But I'm not unhappy
I'll return again some day.

I'm going home without you
I've set you free
I've always needed you more
Than you ever needed me.

And yet I feel unencumbered;
I'm on my own,
Rather glad that the last child
Is out and gone.

Logan, My Five Year Old Great-Grandson

I stooped and kissed him,
Said I love you.
He answered, I love you too,
Grandma, so much.

Those two added words
Mean so much to me.
I love you, Logan.

Noah

Noah is our quiet one,
Always with a smile.
Will he be the antithesis of Logan?
We won't know for a while.
I love you, sweet baby.

Harper, Our Three Year Old

Harper, you amaze me
You say your ABCs,
You recite scripture,
You sing and play with ease.

Truly you are our miracle child.
I love you.

Henleigh

Henleigh, you're a a little sprite.
You are bubbly, joyful,
Giggly, and a mime.
You are Harper's little sister,
Following her all the time.

You are so dear to me.
I love you.

Memories Of Graduating Seniors

Our memories are many
    And very precious too.
As we travel back through the years
    How very fast they flew.

Twice a day a short recess
    Brought instant joy and fun.
Perhaps a game of "hide and seek,"
    Or marbles had begun.

Hopscotch was a favorite game
    To every little girl.
Lots of boys played mumble peg
    While giving knives a whirl.

Then later in junior high
    Boys showed off for the giggly girls
Wearing tank tops or miniskirts
    And carefully crafted curls.

Pretending not aware of them,
    Guys gathered in small groups
Wrote girl's initials on sidewalks
    Strutted around in boots.

'Twas in high school romance began;
  The boys became changed.
Instead of teasing, hands were held
  And even dates arranged.

Exciting times, proms, end of school
  Tempered by future plans
Shall we join the work force, or
  Travel to other lands?

Proverbial road not taken—
  This is the time to choose
For if we take the wrong path now
  There could be much to lose.

As to school days we bid goodbye,
  New beginnings are here.
The life we've been preparing for
  Tonight we know is near.

We've gathered here to say farewell,
  But memory never ends;
We've formed a bond forever close
  Let's always remain friends.

My Friend

There is this man who lives next door
　He brings my mail each day.

Sometimes he even brings me food,
　Carries my trash away.

For all the kindness he shows me
　I never can repay.

Truly, this neighbor is my friend
　What more is there to say?

My Getaway

The incredible beauty of the ocean today
With its green, blue and purple reaching
To the distant horizon
And the incessant overlapping crescendos
        Soothed me.

The walk on the sandy, sea shelled beach
Peopled with sleeping sun bathers,
A group of raucous picnickers,
And happy clam diggers
        Was peaceful.

I abandoned my life at the condo,
Collected a plastic bag of white and
Silver, black and fuchsia striped shells.
Tasted the salt of the rushing white caps
And ground into the sand with my Nikes
        Feeling weightless and free.

Tonight I switched on the TV to catch the
news.
A small ship hit a diver and never knew until
later.
The diver's arm and his spinal column were
severed.
They held his name pending notification.
For a moment the blue green ocean turned
red.
        I felt heavy again.

Never Say, How Are You?

There is this lady in our club
    You do not dare to ask.
She takes the time to list her pains
    It truly is a task.

"You know I really hurt my back
    The time I stumped my toe.
My eyes, they now have cataracts,
    And they give me such woe."

So, on and on she chatters still.
    While listening to her pains,
On other things my mind does dwell—
    "I really hope it rains."

No Remorse

There was a time when childhood dreams
    We thought would all come true.
No goal we thought impossible,
    But how? We had no clue.

Sometimes, when thinking now of then
    Nostalgia fills my heart—
The naiveté, the simple life
    Of which we were a part.

But would I bring it back again,
    Recall those times gone by?
I think not. No, I don't think so,
    But please don't ask me why.

Noble Sacrifice

With war come sorrow, grief and hurt to
    Child, sister, wife or brother,
But may we not forget the pain
    Of the gold star mother.

Some little child may never know
    Touch of a father's hand
And, oh, the pain a mother feels
    We all can understand.

We see the silver in her hair
    The wrinkles in her brow.
She wonders why people must kill
    And how God does allow.

She sits alone and cries for him,
    Goes back in memory.
Once so young and innocent
    He clung there at her knee.

She watched him grow and dreamed about
    What he'd grow up to be.
She never dreamed he'd give his life
    To keep his country free.

What can we say to comfort her,
    Her sorrow to assuage?
We have no guarantee they won't
    Another war engage.

Our only hope for peace is faith,
    So for our leaders pray
That God will draw them to himself
    And they'll not turn away.

We fear that war will always be
    And some will lose their lives
Perhaps we'll know and understand
    The day Jesus arrives.

Nostalgic Thoughts Of Winter And Fall

The exhilaration of fall—
Sweet smoke from burning leaves,
A wind that tickles and shivers,
Brings need for longer sleeves.

Luminous sight of colors bright—
Scarlet, yellow and bronze,
Followed by matted ghost of grass
On peoples' dying lawns.

Autumn's a magic time so brief
Then pallid dusty trees
Signs of winter, runny noses,
Morning frost and light breeze.

Climate changes the appetite,
Winesap apples, peach, and plum.
Field grown pumpkins,
Spicy wassil with rum.

Finally winter in full force
Immobilizes all
Ice-covered trees and power outs
Soon bid good-bye to fall.

First snow, a pristine wonderland,
Skates, sleds and snug warm caps
Or just a book beside the fire
Late night movies perhaps.

Our great creator gives to us
Wonders of each season
And when with sunshine come the storms
We know there's a reason.

Passing Times

When dog days of August were gone,
    And fall was in the air,
Our swimming pool was almost dry,
    But no one seemed to care.

September was a happy time
    For all my friends and me.
With no more cotton to be picked,
    Scales hung under the trees.

School days were merry days for us—
    A rush to greet old friends.
Rowdy and raucous, boys and girls
    Played games that had no ends.

Oh, that was a joyous time,
    One free from grief or pain.
There was a certain innocence
    That one cannot regain.

Preview For Heaven

Last night I dreamed I saw your face
     And heard you speak to me,
Observed your smiling, clear blue eyes,
     Your movements full and free.

All your handicaps were gone.
     You walked so straight and tall
And as you strode across the way
     You didn't limp at all.

I went to you and grasped your face,
     And both your cheeks I kissed.
Then I gazed at that same small grin
     The one I've always missed.

When I awoke, I felt so good,
     Surprisingly, not sad.
I know someday we'll meet again,
     For that I am so glad.

Respectful Decline

Softly, almost silently, the rain falls.
Suddenly, outside a bobwhite calls.
Sleep has eluded me; I'm quite awake.
Feeling compelled, a decision to make.

"There's a job for you here Mom," you said.
As one thing to another had led.
"There's nothing left to keep you there;
Dad's gone and sister wouldn't really care.

Move your things and come to stay,
Then we'll not be so far away.
You'll have your work; give it a try
A new job, a new home and us nearby."

Oh, my children, almost you persuade,
But I must tell you my decision I have made.
I have my own life that I must live,
Here, I fear I'd take more than I could ever
give,

Of your time that's needed for each other
You'd be sacrificing for your mother.
I know the kindness of you both
And to say no I've been loath.

I'll be leaving tomorrow my dears
You'll send me off with hugs and tears.
You'll wave to me there then turn away
To think of the cares and demands of your
day.

You'll call often and send letters and cards
The whole family will send their regards.
Yes, we'll both have space to live out our lives;
Unencumbered by burdens until the end
arrives.

Goodbye my children and thanks a lot
Mail to me the things I've forgot.

Sacrifices

'Twas summer and vacation time,
     Finding a pleasant place
The lovers sat upon a rock.
     They sat there face to face.

The lovely girl with soft green eyes
     Had quite a puzzled look.
Bill took her hand, but dropped his eyes,
     Just sat there by the brook.

"I hate to tell you this," he said.
     "There'll be no June wedding.
You see in June I'll not be here,
     For to war I'm heading."

"Sorry to disappoint you,"
     He turned to her and said.
"I don't know when I will return
     Or if alive or dead."

With pleading eyes, he looked at her
     And softly took her hand,
"Just say that you will wait for me
     And that you understand."

"I'm sorry that we cannot wed
        As we planned in June.
But I will stay and wait for you,
        Please come back to me soon."

Now many years have come and gone
        Since Bill and June were wed
And after raising six children,
        My parents are now dead.

But oft they told of their courtship
        And of that time when war
Strengthened the love already there
        In courtship from afar.

With letters sent both back and forth
        They became truly friends.
They came to know each other well
        That's how the story ends.

Some Mother's Son

The nameless, hopeless and homeless—
    You will see them there,
But no one takes the time to look,
    To help or even care.

I must have passed him many times
    The disconnected man
Walking with crutches, empty sleeves,
    The one who has no plan.

And yet I never stopped to help
    Nor did I ask his name.
Does this dry soul feel no remorse,
    Or just a bit of shame?

They say he died there on the street
    With people all around.
Though his eyes were filled with tears
    No person heard a sound.

They're in the cities everywhere—
    Invisible to us
Just the bag people we ignore
    Who seldom make a fuss.

Some mother's son he must have been.
　Maybe a soldier boy.
Perhaps he once knew happiness
　And had a heart of joy.

We'll read about his death tonight
　And yes, we'll even grieve
For brief moments, the problem then
　To others we will leave.

Suddenly, I'm Old

My Christmas card list is shorter
    It seems most every year.
And for the names I have crossed out,
    I stop and shed a tear.

Where did they go, those friends of old?
    Surely not moved away.
Truly, I know that some have moved
    But most have passed away.

Temporary

Into each heart some sadness comes,
  And for a time there's pain.
But just as sure as our God lives,
  There's sunshine with the rain.

A cheery smile can sunshine bring
  To hearts that have grown cold.
Yes, a bit of encouragement
  To those both young and old.

Hail and thunder come with a storm,
  A rainbow with the rain.
Then, rowdy flowers peeping out
  Make my heart sing again.

I dare not sit alone and pout;
  No pity reaches me.
There's music still within my heart
  And my God smiles with me.

That Certain Smile

Today I strode along the way
The paths where we once trod.
In memory-softened sadness
There I communed with God.

Ever thankful for His blessings
And memories so dear.
I stopped beneath the old oak tree
And felt that you were near.

I thought of our two children
I wish that you could see
And know the people they've become,
How proud I feel you'd be.

And, oh, the little ones so dear
The joy they bring to me,
And if I glimpse a certain smile,
It's your smile that I see.

The love we shared has been passed on,
Yet kept within my heart.
As long as our progeny exists
You'll always be a part.

The Beauty Of Her Smile

I love the beauty of her smile,
  The kindness in her eyes.
Despite that hair so snowy white,
  She's still so very wise.

If she whispers, "I'll pray for you,"
  You know she really cares.
Never does she complain or show
  Burdens she herself bears.

The Death Of Our Class Comedian

You reposed there in a flag-draped casket.
Two musicians played a guitar and a violin
While they softly sang "Go Rest High on the
Mountain."

They buried you with your cream colored
ten gallon hat and recalled
a myriad of stories about the wild,
rambunctious boy you once were.

Where are you?? Surely not
there in that flag draped casket.

The Quiet Man

He sits there alone.
Wonder what he's thinking.
Are his thoughts about days gone by
As the sun is sinking?

Is he recalling days of old,
Times when dreams were new,
Longing to go back to the time
When there was much to do?

Or, is he thinking my back aches,
Gotta get my rest.
I'd guess I'd better call the doc
And go in for a test.

The Simple Life

All brown, it sat upon the angry foam
Quiet and watchful as a distant ship
Taking cargo to places far from home.
Among the waves it seemed to sway and dip
Into the water like a fishing net.
It trapped the fish inside the giant lip;
A quicker meal no man could ever get.

Observing from this quiet peaceful shore,
I thought how simple is the life of him—
A home and food, no need for wall or door
Or worries of a future dark and dim.

I envied him his wild but simple life
Floating watchful, yet with so little strife.

They Still Dance

She lives out in the nursing home;
  Her husband comes each day.
He pushes her around the yard,
  Pauses along the way.

They smell the flowers, pick a few,
  But seldom does she smile.
She asks him, "When can we go home?"
  He answers, "In a while."

Last night he took her to the dance,
  And while the music played,
They waltzed around out on the floor.
  He held her as they swayed.

Slowly, slowly, they danced out there,
  And as I glimpsed her face,
I saw the beauty of her smile,
  The dignity and grace.

Too Late?

Once there was a little boy
    Whose name was Harold Dean.
He gave me a valentine.
    Prettiest I'd ever seen.

He cried big tears for me the time
    His family moved away.
My heart felt sad to lose my friend
    On that regretful day.

Now that was many years ago
    When I last saw my friend.
He called to me, "Goodbye, goodbye
    A letter I will send."

I never heard from him again
    No letter I received,
But those tear were tears of love
    I truly believed

At our school reunion we met
    He said, "You were my girl."
When I saw this old gray haired man,
    He gave my heart a whirl.

To Whom Much Is Given

Out there along the busy street
    An humble beggar sat.
He said, "If you have ought for me,
    Just drop it in the hat."

Quickly, I dipped down in my purse,
    Pulled out a dollar bill.
Then when I dropped it in his hat,
    His eyes with tears did fill.

"Thank you, lady! Bless you my dear."
    The ragged beggar cried.
"Almighty God's blessed me today.
    He's right here by my side."

And then I bowed my head in shame.
    From God I've received much
Could I not have given more to
    The soldier with his crutch??

"For unto whomever much is given,
    Of him shall be much required."
(Luke 12: H 8 B)

Together At Last

Both in their teens the couple were
    The first time that they met,
Just out of school and each unsure,
    No future plans were set.

And though we know they fell in love,
    He said she broke his heart.
She says no, that he broke hers.
    We know that they did part.

Each met and married someone else.
    My, how the time did fly!
Each had a busy, happy life,
    But now and then a sigh—

Sometimes nostalgia would creep in:
    Feelings of time or place.
She saw someone that looked like him.
    One time he glimpsed her face.

The children all grew up and left.
    There was the empty nest.
But so busy their lives still were
    No time to think or rest.

Then suddenly ill health appeared,
    And each one lost a spouse.
There in her condo Shirley remained
    While Bill lived in his house.

Though between them stretched many miles
    And many years have passed—
She called him or he called her?
    Together again at last.

Too Much Fun

You've wined me and dined me
    And shown me around.
We've gone fishing and sightseeing
    And taken in the town.

The Biltmore House we've viewed
    And Caesar's Head.
At the home of Carl Sandburg
    The goats we've fed.

Taking a picnic to Sliding Rock
    We all got wet.
Visiting the forest and a sawmill
    A ranger we met.

In a clear little stream
    We fished for trout.
To catch them was fun
    The children found out.

I love North Carolina
    It's a beautiful state.
But I'm catching that plane for home
tomorrow
    And I hope it's not late.

Trip To Sandburg's Home

I made a pilgrimage last week.
I saw Conemara.
The guide told us much about your life—
Your wife, your children,
Even your favorite drink of honey, tea and
goat's milk.

She said you led a sparse life.
Your tastes were simple.
Your wants were few.
She told us that though you had the means,
Your home was rather stark—lacking richness
and luxury.

She was entirely wrong!
Your home was as I expected.
Everything was plain, simple and lovely.
The view was breathtaking—uncluttered
Like your poetry.

You enriched my knowledge of Abraham
Lincoln
Made me to envision a bustling windy city,
Sparked my curiosity about the hobo's life,
Touched me with compassion for the war
dead,
Calmed me with your picture of the fog
coming in on little cat's feet.

I've known you for so long
Returned to you again and again—
For enlightenment, for pure pleasure and just
to renew acquaintance.
When I felt a vague emptiness, you filled the
vacuum.
Ever I've longed to know you better.

Unexpected Love

This feeling that I have for you
    Came unexpectedly.
Its coming at this time of life
    Is quite a mystery.

My love for you I can't express
    In ordinary words.
It's old, yet new and strange.
    It's like the song of birds.

Or perhaps the rainbow in the sky
    Appearing after rain—
Before you're sure you've seen it there
    It comes and goes again.

I never dreamed I'd know once more
    A love so deep and true.
I didn't think there'd come again
    Another man like you.

But now that you have come my way
    Living once more is sweet.
Doing the little things for you
    My life is made complete.

I need you to protect and keep
    Me always by your side,
And may our love remain as strong
    And sure as the ocean tide.

Taking our marriage vows today
    We begin life anew.
We'll pledge our love forever when
    We say the words "I do".

Why?

Why do some people lean on me,
To me their troubles tell?
Just know that I have troubles too,
On which I hate to dwell.

You do not like your son's new wife,
Perhaps she feels the same,
Or maybe its just because that you
Don't remember her name.

Your husband left you high and dry,
Saying, "Life's just not fun."
Well, lady, why don't you tell him
"For me, life's just begun."

I'm not callous, I have a heart
Sometimes the trouble's real.
Then I ask you to sit right down
And tell me how you feel.

My shoulder's broad and perhaps we
Can cheer each other up
So let us just sit down and try
Over a morning cup.

Hard But Necessary Changes

Heading the list on the scribble, a term I'd learned from my Nova Scotia pupil, was I'm alone; I live alone; I make decisions without the need to consult or consider the opinions of anyone else directly concerned. I, alone decide when and where to go. I decide when, where, what and if to eat. I decide how much money to spend and on what; and concurrently, I decide whether and how much I should save.

All of the above could be good—give one a sense of freedom, of adventure. Before marriage and a partnership in which decisions and responsibilities were shared I would have embraced being free and independent. Now only I am responsible for the care of the farm.

I must remember to keep receipts for income tax purposes. Then there are the endless dates for car tags and insurance, house insurance, property taxes and reading the meter for the rural electric at the farm. There is the butane tank to check periodically and the note on the farm and the cows. So many things that had been shared were now mine alone and I feel overcome with responsibilities. When I forgot to pay my health insurance premium I was terrified that they would cut me off, but then I noticed that I had a grace period.

Next I had to delve into the intricacies of the greatest change that my husband's death brought into my life. I am no longer part of a couple—I am one. And as one I knew there were things, which inevitably were going to be different. These people were still my friends, but now I was their friend with a problem. I am a widow, a person who lost her husband. Many of them included me on outings, invited me to visit "anytime" and called me frequently, at first.

However, I noticed that I wasn't asked to their homes when other couples were visiting. Oh, if I happened to call and others were there, they'd say, "We're playing bridge, come over," or "Joe and Sue are here and we're chewing the fat. Would you like to join us?" They sounded as if they meant it, but they'd not thought to (or meant to) ask me sooner. I knew I must come to an acceptance and try to understand my new status. If I wanted to avoid feeling offended, I also must accept the changed circumstances fate had brought to my life.

After this, I decided to face another fact that bore such a nibbling fear with it that I persistently pushed it to the back of my mind. This was the fact that I was entirely responsible for my own physical and financial well-being. With the final admission of the full reality of this, I realized that I must be less careless with my health, and must be fully aware of the consequences if I ignored these facts.

Never again, unless I remarried, would there be that comfortable, secure feeling that I was being taken care—that things would be O.K. whether I kept my job or stayed at home. Oh, I would hate to lose my job because of an economic crisis or some other unforeseeable circumstance, but that was something I hadn't worried about before because I had a partner who made a good living.

I knew beyond a doubt this had changed. I loved teaching, reveled in it sometimes. This was a part of my life that had been important for a long while. Why should anything be different now? I wasn't sure why, but it was.

Something else must be dealt with. It was time, to be quite honest with myself, to examine my feelings, face them, and make some decisions. This was perhaps the hardest part of all and one that had not been a problem for so long. It was, say it, face it—my sexuality. It surprised me, quite honestly, to discover these feelings within myself. I thought that part of my life was over. We'd had those first years of awkward uncertainty, passion, sometimes anger, unable to communicate without painful embarrassment—then our love matured. At what point in time, I couldn't say, but there was a melding of feelings, naturalness, a trusting that was joyful and (old-fashioned) sweet. Strange as it might seem to some I felt our love grow into friendship.

I worked days, often my husband worked late evenings but I had never felt alone. He'd call—often hurriedly between tasks—but

almost always he'd ask, "How was your day?" and he meant it. When
he was tired, or worried, I would sense it immediately.

We had a sort of mental shorthand. And we had our little games,
too—years ago a doctor prescribed sex more often as a solution to
pain from a prostate problem. When we'd almost forgotten the origin
of the joke, he'd ask, "Shall I take my medicine tonight?" or I would
turn coy and say, "Watch out, honey, or I'll throw your medicine
away." There were a million shared experiences, some not directly
connected with sex, but all interwoven with the closeness, and feeling
of oneness we felt for each other.

He worried when his illness first began to manifest itself in a
physical way, and I assured him that it wasn't important; that only
his being cared for, only the relief of his pain was of paramount
importance to me.

The last few times we attempted physical intimacy was terrifying
for me because of my fear for him. I was relieved when he ceased
thinking about it. My time was entirely taken up with my consuming
concern for his well being.

I met Bill three or four weeks after John's death and was
quite shocked when I felt a physical attraction for him. He was a
businessman that I had dealings with, and was quite surprised when
he called me. He didn't know my being a widow was a recent thing
and backed off, not pressing me, but keeping in touch. Although I
was quite emphatic in telling him it was too soon to go out socially,
I, too kept in touch with him through the necessity for our business
contact. And then there was the fact that he called on one pretext or
another, or just to talk.

Other things were happening too. Two other men called. One,
a widower, whose wife had been my friend, called frequently just to
offer friendship in my time of need. He called several times, but never
made an overture. Another, a farmer, told me frankly that he had lost
his wife and was looking for another. He said, "I saw you recently
and thought I'd ask—will you go out to supper with me?" I gently
told him that I was busy with my children, suppressing the urge to
be facetious when he prefaced his request with "Do you ever go out?"
Then to my surprise, an old flame called to express his condolences
and told me to drop by and see him the next time I was in the city.
This was all so new, so unexpected and so disturbing.

Suddenly the holidays were upon me. My feeling of loss loomed large at this time. I would feel devastated at times, overcome with almost unbearable grief. Then I'd have this unexplainable anticipation. It was a long period of inactivity, of tight anxiety. Suddenly I felt driven to experience something new, something forbidden. I called Bill and invited him to accompany me to a school function. He seemed pleased at the invitation and I half enjoyed the evening—then refused another "date" with him; saying I was too busy. The whole experience brought a vague feeling of disappointment and guilt.

As I pondered on this new aspect of my life, I felt so vulnerable. Then I asked—would I ever truly be attracted, seriously attracted to another man, and if I were, could I trust my feelings?" Definitely, at this point in my life, I am not ready to face and resolve all the problems that question poses.

Thinking on these things, I realize that things are changing, have changed already to a certain degree.

When the children were young and demanding and John was working so hard, I longed for, and sometimes stole for myself a bit of solitude now and then. It was my way of gaining privacy even in the presence of others—while driving, watching television, or even in a crowd of people.

I had a practice of slipping into myself—just an inner quietness, a private communion within—nothing mystical or supernatural. Becoming aware of this, John was usually indulgent and teased me a bit about not being "with them." Occasionally he became irritated, demanding of my attention, especially on our travels when he, the ever practical one, wanted my full participation in seeing and discussing such mundane things as government-backed experimental corn fields or huge cattle feed lots.

Loving him as I did, and appreciative of his tolerance of my penchant for museums and "restored" homes, searching for lovely depression ware and other antiques; I allowed myself to come back to the present.

After John's death, I was afraid to be alone—sought the company of people constantly. There were so many loving friends, my children, my wonderful brothers. There was no dearth of invitations, of places to go—yet I had not taken time to be alone with myself or with God.

I'd somehow put God's work on hold and pushed to the back of my mind all the sorrow and unhappiness; I'd been running—constantly running.

Now, at last, I'm beginning to enjoy being alone again. I've made one or two nice friends who like me, were alone for some reason or another. I've renewed my interest in painting, in needlework and my great passion for reading. I'm doing volunteer work again. It's a start, at least. More important it is a realistic start.

⚜

The Games We Used To Play

My friend Norma Gammill's eleven-year old granddaughter, Chloe, is spending the summer with Norma and her grandfather Jay. Knowing how quickly children grow up, Norma wanted to make this summer very special.

We began to reminisce about the games we played as children. Chloe is delighted with her newly acquired knowledge. She's assured us that she can't wait to explain all she's learned to her sixth grade classmates back in Pennsylvania.

I started remembering the games we played when we were children. Then my brothers and friends got in on the fun.

We've come up with about fifty games and still more are tickling our minds. I hope the games included bring back memories of fun and friends.

Red Rover

Using two captains, choose up sides. Each side forms a line. Each line stands about twenty feet from the other.

The captain, or a delegated player polls his team and the name of an opponent is chosen. In unison the team calls out, "Red Rover, Red Rover, let whomever come over.

The players grip hands very tightly while the chosen opponent runs as fast as he can, trying to break through the line. If he breaks the line, he chooses a player to return with him. If he doesn't break through, he remains on his opponent's side. The game ends when one side has all or most of the players.

11 The Needle's Eye

Appoint two players to be captains. They secretly name themselves. We used such names as "golden apples" and "silver oranges"— it's up to the captains. The captains form an arch with their arms and hands. The players run through the arch singing, "Needles Eye, the Dust Supply, the thread that runs so truly.

Many a beau have I let go because I wanted youly.

Mother taught me how to sew and how thread the needle.

Every time I take a stitch, pop goes the weasel!"

When they say, "Pop goes the weasel," the captains catch the player that happens to be beneath the arch. They grab him, take him away from the other players and whisper, "Would you rather be a golden apple or a silver orange?" Whichever he chooses, he gets behind the captain with that name and holds on.

When all the players have been caught, they hold on behind their captains and pull with all their might. The side that falls first is the loser and the side that is left standing is the winner.

III Go In And Out The Windows

The players form a circle. Choose two players to go under the players' hands. (Oh yes, players are holding hands, lifted up). As one player chases the other, the players sing, "Go in and out the windows, Go in and out the windows, Go in and out the windows—For we have gained this day."

If the player who started has caught the other by the time the little diddy ends, the other player is it. If not the first player becomes it.

The one who is it goes to the center, and is blindfolded. As the players sing he marches around the circle.

Players sing: "Go forth and choose you lover. Go forth and choose you lover. Go forth and choose your lover. For we have gained this day."

When the verse ends, the blindfold is removed and the player of the opposite sex nearest to him goes to the center with him. He kneels before the one he has chosen. They cross arms and hold hands.

In the fifth grade we girls got quite a thrill from this. The boys acted a bit reluctant.

As the two players moved their clasped hands back and forth the others sang: "I'll measure my love to show you. I'll measure my to show you. I'll measure my love to show you. For we have gained this day."

When the verse ends, the player arises, begins to wave to the partner as the players sing: "Good-bye, I hate to leave you. Good-bye I hate to leave you. Good-bye I hate to leave you. For we have gained this day."

The player left standing is "it" and the game begins all over again.

IV Three Deep

Form two circles, drop hands, leaving two players standing in front of each other. Choose two players to be "it." One chases the other as they run around the circles. The one being chased stops in front of a player, making "three deep." The one on the outside, then tries to elude the one chasing him. If he gets caught, then he becomes the chaser.

V Ball And Jacks

Played with a small rubber ball and jacks, this game can progress from very simple moves to quite intricate ones.

First round of the game a player picks up a jack and catches the ball with the same hand until she has picked up all of the jacks. This goes from ones (we pronounced it oneses), then twos, threes, etc.

The second round is called "eggs in the basket," where one picks up the jacks, puts them in the other hand, then catches the ball. Just as above, a player goes through ones, twos, threes, etc.

Next, there is the "pigs in the barn." A player simply makes a small barn, or opening with her hand on the floor. She throws the ball in the air, pushes the jacks in the barn with her hand, then catches the ball. This requires a lot of dexterity.

If a player progresses this far, there is also "crack the eggs," and "sheep over the fence.

In "sheep over the fence" the player lays her forearm on the floor then has to maneuver the jacks around the "fence" before catching the ball.

As children we girls got hours of fun from playing this game.

VI Jumping Rope

There were two kinds of jumping rope. Many of us had our own individual jumping rope. Usually the handles were red and one handle was a whistle. Sometimes we jumped, alternating with skipping. We could do this in groups or alone.

The game I enjoyed the most was when we used a longer rope, with two players turning the rope for us. They usually started out rather slowly, then became faster and faster.

We had some little rhymes we chanted. One of them was the following:

"Mother, Mother, shall I die?

"Yes, my Dear, but do not cry.

"How many years shall I live?"

Next, we would begin jumping and counting. When the player missed, that ended the counting.

A second game we played with a long rope was a game of competition. We'd choose sides, then one at a time we'd run through the turning rope, skipping just one time each time we ran through. As a player failed to make it, she dropped out. The team with fewer mistakes was the winner.

VII Bobbing For Apples

Often done at our Halloween carnival, bobbing for apples could be great fun. Our teacher would bring a small washtub, fill it with water and add some apples, then we'd take time about trying to pick up an apple with our mouth or teeth. Back then I don't believe we were too concerned with hygiene.

Another game played with apples was one where they'd tie an apple by the stem with a string, then hang it. Standing with your hands behind you, you tried to catch the apple with your mouth or teeth. If you caught the apple you were allowed to eat it.

VIII Roll The Hoop

Dad would take an old broomstick and nail an old Prince Albert tobacco can on the end of the stick, curving it just a little.

We'd take a small hoop or wheel, then race each other pushing the wheel in front of us as we ran. The one who reaches "goal" first was the winner. This game could be played at home between two or more players or at recess at school, there could be teams.

IX Barrel Walk And Barrel Ride

The barrel walk was simple. Two people climbed up on individual barrels and tried to walk on them without falling. If they were racing, and one fell off he could jump back on and keep trying to go faster than his opponent.

My brother, Don Eldridge tells me barrel racing is strictly for boys and that protective headgear is needed. When I demurred about it being just a boy's game he said, "Well and also tomboys."

To do a barrel roll, a barrel would be taken to the top of a hill, a player would hunker up inside the barrel, then yell, "Let her roll!"

The other players would give the barrel a shove, letting it take off down the hill. If a rock or bunch of briars happened to stop it, they took off after it and gave it another shove.

Landing at the foot of the hill, the passenger often felt quite bruised. It's not clear to me why, but I got quite a rush when I tried it. I don't remember trying it but once.

Naomi Tomlinson is a retired teacher. She has had numerous poems, articles and short stories published in magazines and the local newspaper.

Last May her book, The Rhymes and Rhythms of My Life was published.

She has had the honor of reading several of her poems at the university in Seattle, Washington.

Poem

By Leroy Dority

My Wife

By Leroy Dority

When this world looked dark and gray
　　Things seemed bad and I can say
The future held nothing new,
　　Until God gave me you.

You drove darkness out of my life
　　When you consented to be my wife.
You put sunlight into my heart
　　Which gave me happiness and a new start.

Your eyes would dim the brightest star
　　And shows your love wherever you are.
You have a smile that's sweeter by far
　　That had made you what you are.

You bore me three sons who we love so dear
　　And a daughter that's beyond compare.
And for these I can only say
　　Without you, there'd been no other way.

No matter what the years may hold
　　My dream has come true, and you should
know
Whatever comes along that's new
　　My love is now, and ever for you.

Leroy Dority wrote this poem fifty years ago for his wife, Betty. The last eight years of her life were spent in the Heritage Village Home, where Leroy visited her every day. She passed away August 20, 2012.

He now spends part of each day doing volunteer work at the Home. He is greatly appreciated by the staff and loved by all the patients.

Poem

By Lori Eikel

My Brother's House

by Lori Eikel

I stop by when I'm in town.
He's not there now.
His imprint is lying on the sofa,
Reclining in the cushions.
The contour of his body visible.

Sweating,

I asked for a T-shirt to put on,

Preferably,

One of his, my brother's.

My need was necessary today,
To be able to sit in his impression on the sofa,
To hold his newborn son.
To comfort and cuddle his daughters.
Paint little fingernails, kiss little toes.
Smooth and braid their hair.

Lon was their father's name, my youngest brother.
When he was eleven, I remember he would say,
"Just call me the Lonz," as he flipped up both
Thumbs and said "heeey." His playful ocean eyes,
(my color). Blonde careless hair, so fine and
sweet-looking.

I feel comfort in my brother's house,
On my brother's sofa,
Loving my brother's children,
Wearing my brother's T-shirt.
I miss my brother's life.

Lori Eikel enjoys photography, reading, and writing poetry. The current highlight of her life is a brand new baby granddaughter.

Poems and Short Stories

By Judy Goodspeed

For Better Or Worse

by Judy Goodspeed

It's three in the morning; I'm packing your bag.
Don't want you to leave, but know not to nag.
Just married a week and now you must go
With Everett and Dick to the Denver rodeo.

For better or worse, that's what we said
But nobody mentioned this half-empty bed.

Two years of marriage, a son on the way
Time for the hospital but you can't stay.
You're leading the average at Fort Worth.
So you have to miss your first baby's birth.

For better or worse, that's what we said
But nobody mentioned this half-empty bed.

The cows are out. Cody has colic.
If I drank I'd be an alcoholic.
The phone rings, you're coming home.
Two wonderful days and then you're gone.

For better or worse, that's what we said
But nobody mentioned this half-empty bed.

The days are too short the nights are too long.
I cry every time I hear a sad song.
Don't know how much loneliness I can take.
Perhaps this marriage is a total mistake.

For better or worse, that's what we said
But nobody mentioned this half-empty bed.

Just when I decide I've had enough.
That the life of a rodeo wife is too tough.
You walk through the door as handsome as sin,
Open your arms, grin that lopsided grin.
And that's when better starts over again.

Mama Tried

by Judy Goodspeed

When I was young and carefree,
My mother said to me,
"You'd best learn to cook and sew."
"Okay Mom," I'd reply and off I'd go,

To ride or fish or play ball,
To quail and duck hunt in the fall.
I loved to read and visit with friends
There was no time to cook or mend.

"You'd best spend time in the kitchen," Mother
would say.
"I will Mom, some other day.
"I'm off to hunt arrowheads in the field,
"Then I should put new line on my reel.

"I need to fish and shoot a few hoops,
"Ride with Dad and throw some loops.
"I love to have fun, run and play
"Doubt that I have time to cook today."

The years have flown and I never had time
To heed the words of that Mother of mine.
I never go hungry, but two husbands have fled.
I guess they grew tired of peanut butter and bread.

I can't sew a seam without making a mistake,
So I do my hemming with masking tape.
My pots have no handles; my oven won't light.
Those who enter my kitchen cry out in fright.

Guess you can say I'm old and carefree,
But that doesn't bother me.
Others have offered advice, given up and sighed,
In the words of Merle Haggard, "Mama tried."

A Stinky Adventure

by Judy Goodspeed

"A skunk can't spray if its back feet are off the ground," I heard Mr. Jones say as I walked up to join Dad who was sitting with the spit and whittle group.

"How can you grab a skunk's tail and get his feet up before he sprays you?" I asked.

"Like this," he said as he pulled my ponytail up.

All of the old timers laughed and even Dad chuckled a little. Well Mr. Jones had just made me mad, and I would show him that I wasn't afraid to test his theory.

I puzzled over the skunk scene knowing there was no way you could approach one from the front and definitely not from behind. Determined to find out if the saying was true I asked my neighbor George to help me come up with a skunk catcher.

George said, "Check with me Friday."

Friday after school I rode my bike to George's house and raced into his shop. He handed me a gadget unlike anything I'd seen. He had taken an old cane, shortened it and cut a groove down one side. A stiff wire was held in the groove by strips of tin. At the top, near the handle, the wire had a hoop so you could pull it with your finger. When you pulled the wire, it took the slack out of a circular spring at the bottom.

"This is great. Thanks George," I said as I pulled the hoop.

"You don't get sprayed," George warned.

"Not a chance. I'll be in a tree."

I ran to say hi to Thelma, George's wife. She was baking chocolate chip cookies. I ate a couple with a glass of cold milk and carried some home with me. Sonny, my brother, appeared out of nowhere when I parked my bike behind the smokehouse. "What's that thing?" he asked.

"This thing is to catch a skunk by the tail so I can lift his back feet off the ground. They can't spray if their back feet are off the ground."

"You're crazy."

"Mr. Jones says it'll work."

"If you believe him, you really are crazy. What's in the bag, skunk bait?"

Before I could answer, he'd snatched the bag and grabbed a cookie.

"I'm going to tell Mom," I said.

"Go ahead, and I'll tell her about your skunk catching plan."

It cost me three cookies to keep him quiet. Sonny walked away with final words of wisdom, "You'll have to shave your head to get the smell out of all that hair."

"I'm not going to get sprayed!"

"That well water sure is cold," he called over his shoulder.

I'd begged Mom for years to put him up for adoption. She always laughed and said, "You'd miss him."

I found a rope and threw it over a limb so I could climb up the big pecan tree that stood at the edge of our yard. One low hanging limb was just right for me to sit or lie on and wait for my prey.

Every day after I finished drying dishes, I scampered to my tree. I waited and watched until dark. Several days passed and I was getting discouraged when I heard Dad tell Mom a skunk was eating the horse's sweet feed. The next afternoon I sprinkled sweet feed around the base of the tree and under my limb.

That evening perched on my limb I waited for some kind of activity. Just about dark something moved in the weeds north of my tree. Watching and listening, I quietly picked up my skunk catcher. Then I reached into my pocket, and fished out a rock to throw so the skunk would raise its tail. At long last, a black nose poked through the weeds. I held my breath as little black eyes looked all around. I zeroed in on every move the skunk made. Feeling secure the skunk began to sniff the sweet feed. It nibbled its way under the limb I sat on.

When it was directly under me, I dropped a rock in front of it. Sure enough up came the tail. Quick as a blink, I stuck the spring over the skunk's tail, and pulled the hoop as I lifted. I heard a squeak. An odor of rotten eggs and burning rubber hit me with a force that could have stopped an elephant. Dropping the skunk catcher I grabbed the limb to keep from falling out of the tree. Rough bark scraped the skin off my arms and face. My eyes burned like fire. While I dangled from the limb, I watched not one but three skunks escape into the woods. I was in big trouble. I didn't even know which skunk was guilty!

Mom was in the kitchen when I opened the back door. I must have looked a mess because she started toward me asking, "What happened?" Then she stopped. One hand covered her nose. "Get outside," she said, not too kindly.

Sonny piped, "I told you, you'd get sprayed."

I headed for the well house, dreading the cold water and worrying that Mom would shave off my hair. She doused me with vinegar, rinsed that off with cold water, scrubbed my hair with some kind of animal shampoo, and threatened to do bodily harm to my friend George.

One thing for sure, next Saturday I would find Mr. Jones and stay as close to him as I could all afternoon.

Judy Goodspeed is a retired teacher and author. She lives on the family farm and enjoys reading, writing and fishing.

Poem

By J.D. Hess

Love's Tempest

By Jerrold (J. D.) Hess

Take my love, the wind
    And wrest it from my heart
        Send it whirling o'er the mountains
            To the sea.

There plunge it to the depths,
    With wild and blinding force
        Then leave it churning, blasting
            To be free.

Faith! Let it burst out, top
    The waves in silv'ry swirls,
        And, riding on their crests, glide
            To the shore.

Surf! Smash it to the rocks
    Sea! Air it to the sky
        Then catch it, fair wind, once more
            To thy breast.

Then wing it to my love's
    Sweet garden, in the sun
        And in soft, warm breezes, lay it
            To her face.

J.D. Hess was born and raised in Arizona but now lives in Oklahoma. He comes from a musical family. His mother was an opera singer and he has been a musician – singer, drummer and poet – for over fifty years.

Short Stories

By Johnnie Wingo

Learning The Language

I was settin under the mulberry tree playin house with a corn husk doll named Martha Jane and a porcelain headed doll named Josephine.

Martha Jane was too stiff to set down and Josephine was too limber to set up at the table I had made out of an apple crate. Martha Jane's right arm flew off when I shook her and Josephine's eyes rolled back in her head when I slapped her. Mama always scolded me bad when things like that happened, so I picked up Josephine, meaning to go ask Pa if he could fix her eyes before Mama got wind of what had happened.

I got to the barnyard just in time to see Pa go out the south gate driving the mules that was hitched to the breaking plow.

I snagged my dress tail when I crawled under the bobwire fence and knew I was in trouble again. Ever dress I owned had been mended several times, which was Mama's fault to my way of thinking. There was half a dozen pairs of blue overalls that my brothers had outgrowed laying around the house just going to waste. I'd tried to get Mama to let me wear them, but she wouldn't hear of it, on account of it not being ladylike. Just thinking about it got me aggravated and I decided to take off my shoes and go barefooted, which was another thing she didn't allow me to do.

I'd meant to catch up to Pa before he got started breaking up the new ground, but by the time I got there I could see that he wasn't in the mood to be interfered with. I hid behind some jimson weeds, meaning to take a lesson in breaking ground because I aimed to be a farmer myself someday even if I was a girl.

It seemed like it was taking Pa an awful long time to get started breaking ground. First he sighted over his thumb at a pecan tree at the far end of the field then pointed the plow in that direction. He tied the ends of the reins together, swung one side over his right shoulder and the other under his left arm. Then he took hold of the plow handles, tipped the plowshare down just a little bit and said real polite like, "Git up."

The mules heads was hanging down like they was studying the ground for news, and they didn't appear to hear. Pa said it again a little louder and not near as polite. Tom switched his tail at a horse fly and Tobe lifted his tail and broke wind, but neither one of them moved a step.

Pa turned loose of one plow handle, flapped the reins hard and yelled "Git up Tom, Git up Tobe" which done the trick as far as getting the mules into action, but turning loose of the plow handle looked to be a serious mistake. The plow gouged a deep hole in the ground, then turned on its side and slid along the ground for a good ten feet.

Pa was jumping along behind, holding on to the plow with one hand and pulling back on the reins with the other.

"Whoa, Tom! Whoa Tobe! Hold up there you infernal jackasses."

Well, I'm here to tell you it was the most exciting thing I'd ever seen. Some of my brothers had been to the county fair one time, and bragged of it often, but I couldn't imagine that it was any more fun than what I was seeing.

It had come to me one time that mayhap Pa wasn't what you'd call a natural born farmer. Once he mended the harness so good that it took him most of the morning to get the mules untangled. Another time he fixed the front gate and we've never been able to open it again.

I asked him once if he had ever thought about being something different, maybe a teacher or a store keeper. How did he come to be a farmer, anyhow?

He pondered over the matter for a spell, then said he believed it was a matter of mistaken identity. Some city fellers went out hunting and mistook the stork for a duck and shot it down. Had he been delivered to his natural birthplace he might have become a riverboat gambler on the Mississippi, or a gold miner in California, or a badge-carrying sheriff out in the wild west.

I remembered that talk whilst I was watching Pa struggle with the mules, and I thought it was a sad thing that some folks ended up in a place where they wasn't meant to be.

Pa had pulled the mules to a stop, lined up the plow with the pecan tree yet again, and said "Git up" in the meanest voice I'd ever heard him use. Tom set right off at a steady pace, but Tobe was skittish. He'd lag back a while, then run forward to overtake Tom and try to pass him up, which he couldn't do, on account of them being in double harness.

Pa's language was a wonder to behold. "Move out there, you dang blasted buzzard bait. Pick up them feet, Tom, you blue bellied son of a bottom land whore. Slow down, Tobe, you sorry son of a low-bred cayuse." Pa wasn't much of a talker around the house, and I had never suspected that he knew such a vast number of words.

I looked back toward the house to see if Mama was in earshot. She once washed Jimmy's mouth out with soap for saying nothing stronger than "Dadbern it" when the cat carried in a dead snake and laid it on the foot of his bed. The trouble with dead snakes is that they won't quit wiggling til the sun goes down, and I could see how Jimmy let out a bad word without meaning to.

The mules finally settled down to their jobs and Pa left off cussing them and spent some time rebuking the Republicans, the President, the WPA and the fate that had made him a farmer in the first place.

We was coming up the end of the row, and Pa seemed to be getting might agitated about something. He kept shifting his hands from the plow handle to the reins and back again, muttering under his breath. The mules didn't appear to notice til the last minute that there was a bob wire fence in front of them. Tom swung left and Tobe pulled to the right, then they switched directions and bumped bellies in the middle.

Pa was yelling all the time: "Whoa Tom! Gee Tobe! Move over there, Tom. Haw! Gee! Haw!" Tom grew stiff legged and Tobe's legs turned to rubber and the plow dipped in and out of the ground digging deep holes that Pa kept falling into. By the time Pa finished turning around and got the mules headed back down the field the end of the row looked like a hog waller.

When I allowed it was safe to come out of hiding I had to run to catch up with them for the mules was stepping out fast now that the barn was before them. Pa kept up a steady stream of cuss words and I listened close so as not to miss a single one.

The mules put on another good show at the next turn around, for they could see the barn and the feed trough and meant to go there in spite of Pa. I hid behind a patch of cuckleburrs till Pa got them headed out again, then I drifted on back to the house, reciting to myself all the best cuss words I had overheard Pa say.

I knew I wouldn't be allowed to use them for a good many years, but it give me a lot of satisfaction to have them. I expect it was much the same way Mama must have felt when she went down into the cellar and counted the jars of goods she had stored up for the future.

Sharecropper's Daughter

Pa came upon me one day while I was settin under a shade tree making mud pies.

"Come along with me," he said, "and I'll show you how pigs does that."

So I followed after him down to the creek where he dipped up a bucket of water. He carried it over to the pig pen and poured it on the ground and the pigs came running and squealing and begun to roll around in the mud. Pa went back to the creek and got a second bucketful and poured it right on top of them, which pleasured them no end. I saw right away that it was a heap more fun than making mud pies and asked if I might try it.

Pa said no at first, he figured it was more of a man's job, and he wasn't sure if a girl could handle it. He gave in though, when I begun to whine and get teary-eyed.

"I reckon I'll turn the job over to you if you'll promise not to carry more than four buckets a day. And if you take on the job you must keep it up, for the pigs will come to depend on you."

So I promised solemn, and kept my word, although at first it was so much fun that I couldn't hardly stand to quit at four bucketfuls a day. Later on, when the job began to get wearisome, the pigs would commence to carry on if I didn't show up and they were always so glad to see me that I hadn't the heart to turn them down.

There are some folks that think pigs aren't very smart, but I reckon they haven't had the pleasure of knowing any personally.

Pa said it was often that way, that folks formed negative opinions on things that they haven't had any experience of. It was his belief, and he taught it to me, that a person should never pass judgment on a thing until he has tried it for himself.

Pa got to be real good about letting me try new things. Over the years he allowed me to gather eggs, shell corn for the chickens, carry in stove wood and drive the cows in from the pasture.

Though he said he hated to give it up, the day came when he turned the milking over to me, but only because his hands had stiffened up with the rheumatism. When he saw how good I did he said he was sorry that he hadn't let me have the job before because I was so much better at it than him.

I took pleasure in everything Pa could be talked into letting me do until he said one day that he guessed I was big enough to be allowed to hoe corn.

I was in the field the next morning while the grass was still wet with dew, and my pleasure in the job dried up about the time the dew did. I could recognize a cuckleburr and a jimson weed, but Johnson grass bears a strong resemblance to a young stalk of corn, and trying to tell the difference slowed me down a right smart. I had turned down Mama's offer to loan me her pink poke bonnet, and before long the sun was bearing down mighty heavy on my head.

Pretty soon I began to figure it to be nigh about noontime, so I looked at the sun and saw that it couldn't have been no more than ten o'clock. So I hoed some more, and looked again, but the sun hadn't hardly moved at all. I must have looked at the sun a dozen times before Mama hollered me in to eat. By then I had begun to form a clear picture of what the preacher meant when he sermonized about eternity in Hell.Now my folks weren't given to complaining, and I never meant to do so myself, but when Pa asked me how I liked the job I told him the plain truth.

"I just can't find any pleasure in it, Pa. I know it must be done, but I've tried it and I reckon that gives me the right to say that I just don't care for it at all. It's the lonesomest job in the world and I estimate that by the time I reach the far side of the field the corn on this side will be ready for picking. That's how slow I am. I just don't seem to have any talent for it."

I flung down my fork and went out behind the henhouse to sulk for a spell. I kicked the hound when he tried to comfort me, shoved a settin hen off her nest, throwed corn cobs at the red rooster and just generally spread my misery all over the barnyard.

After a while I began to feel sorry about the way I had acted and went to tell Pa so, but he was riding down the road on the saddle-broke mule, so I picked up my hoe and went back to the field where I spent the longest afternoon of my life. I thought I might die from the heat and boredom, and wished I would, and made plans to run off with the circus next time it came to the county seat.

I went to the supper table looking as pitiful as possible, with blistered hands, sore feet, a cooked brain and sunburned nose, and right off Pa said the words I had hoped to hear. "You needn't go back to hoeing tomorrow. I went out today and rounded up some hired hands to come in next week and finish the job," he said.

Which might have been the end of the whole thing, had he not gone on to say that he saw he had expected too much of a young girl. I had been thinking the same thing myself, but hearin him say it didn't set too well. He worried over the subject all through supper, saying how sorry he was that he had overloaded me, and my hackles begun to rise. When he finally got around to saying that a girl just couldn't rightly be expected to do as much as a boy I flat out told him he was wrong.

"You haven't never give me a job I couldn't handle, and I'll be blamed if you're going to take this one away from me."

Next morning I asked Mama for the use of her bonnet and went out to make up with the hound. He was an agreeable old soul; he forgave me right off and I coaxed him to the field with me for company.

I figured my mistake the previous day had been to worry about the overall size of the job, so I determined to keep my head down and never look back to see how little I had done or how much there was yet ahead of me.

To keep my brain from addling I recited every Bible verse and poem I had ever been made to memorize, and went on to make up a few of my own. I recited the multiplication table through the nines and taught myself through times twelve though I might have made a few mistakes here and there.

The dog took considerable interest in the verses and poems, but he mostly slept through the times tables and when I tried singing he grew so mournful that I had to give it up. It has been a great sorrow in my life that I can't carry a tune in a tow sack.

I finished the last row one evening an hour before sundown, shouldered the hoe like a rifle and marched off to the house like a soldier returning from a hard fought battle.

Pa saw me coming and walked out to the edge of the field to meet me. He said I had done a fine job, that he didn't know of any man or boy in the county who could have done it better, and he begged my pardon for misjudging me.

That was ever the way it was with Pa, when he was wrong he always owned right up to it, and I have always been proud to be known as the daughter of Tom Sawyer.

Johnnie Wingo is a farmer's daughter who writes stories about growing up on a farm back in the days when there was no electricity or running water and all the work was done by hand.

"It's a lot more fun writing about it than it was living it."

Edwards Brothers Malloy
Thorofare, NJ USA
June 5, 2015